THE
CONSOLATIONS

Also by John W. Evans

Young Widower: A Memoir

THE CONSOLATIONS

Poems by John W. Evans

Winner of the 2013 Trio Award

Evans, John W.
1ˢᵗ edition.

ISBN: 978-0-9855292-4-6
Library of Congress Control Number: 2013942080

Interior Layout by Lea C. Deschenes
Cover Design by Dorinda Wegener
Cover Art by Rachel Burgess
Editing by Dorinda Wegener

Printed in Tennessee, USA
Trio House Press, Inc.
Fernandina Beach, FL
Ponte Vedra Beach, FL

To contact the author, send an email to submissions@triohousepress.org

*To Cait, for your love and care and patience,
for your understanding, and for our beautiful boys,
all more than I could ever have imagined.*

The Consolations

THE CONSOLATIONS

YEARS

Do we derive our comfort from the hope that you will hear us?
—Augustine, *Confessions* (3.10)

MONTHS

Part-Time

One Month

The first job you take after your wife dies suddenly
will be mindless, easy to manage, with flexible hours:
the job you've spent your whole life avoiding.
It bores you to tears. You think, *Ten hours a week*
and it doesn't even cover the therapy, pills, and gas.
The clerks at the all-night grocery rotate shifts:
sunflowers shrinking into the vase on her desk,
an altar of trinkets, her photo in a simple frame.
In the end, what more is there to say
about these long afternoons when the sun
stands solstice in between the coming and going,
you in your black tee-shirts and stain-resistant chinos,
as whole weeks announce the end of summer,
a full moon dimmed by the glow of the city,
these nights when the neighbors fire great floodlights
at the lawn beneath their windows?

ECLOGUE

Twenty-Two Months

Rent in the neighborhood is dropping.
Rent everywhere is dropping. Can you spare
a little CHANGE,
asks the sign where my bank,
merging with the bank across the street,
fails. I want to own land in my country.
I want to make my place in this city certain.
The fish in the bar next to the laundromat:
do they know the limits of their translucent world?
When my wife died I thought,
All within us praise His holy name.
His power and glory ever more proclaimed.
Even then I knew that life didn't really end,
that it would fissure into two places,
inside and out. The woman I love now
distinguishes absence from loss.
When there is no fog on a nearby hill
we walk through her old neighborhood
to the city's highest point.

Scale

Nineteen Months

That spring I pursued the other side of anxiety.
I measured exact distances wherever I went:
days since your death, weeks until your birthday,
how many steps it took to cross the interstate park
where every three weeks the billboard changed
until Oscar season. How I missed being in love.
How I wanted to explain: I miss being in love.
The night your brother stopped talking to his wife
I knew it meant I'd have to choose sides.
I sat dumb and silent, smiling weakly at everything.
At the climbing gym he got faster up the hard-candy steps,
his fingertips smooth and dull. Your nephew
and I registered online an animatronic vulture
whose virtual home contained separate rooms
for each family member. The week he finally
blew out his back your brother slept on the sofa.
He said he didn't want to wake the kids.
Each time he hobbled to the medicine cabinet
the television drowned out his sighs and moans.
I sat in my room listening carefully to music
I knew would make me weep.
Sleeping pills erased the dark room.
Through the window his truck engine turned over four times
before it began its morning loop around the city.

THERE ARE NO WORDS

Six Weeks

Her last few years in the house
my grandmother mastered a capacity for preserving foodstuffs,
uncertain what would be lost, or when.
When we emptied her deep freezer we found
butter from 1994, hogsheads of ice cream, enough lemon
  concentrate
to ceviche the lake where I fished with my grandfather.
He was a quiet man who was always doing nice things.
During his wake my father delivered the sort of eulogy
I want to write now but I don't know where to start.

The week of your funeral,
a poet wrote to tell me, *There are no words,*
and I thought, *Isn't that your job?* Don't you spend all day
finding *words* for situations, fascinations, strangers? Poems for
  the dead
are called elegies. The best elegies rattle around anthologies
like lost guitar picks, suggesting a kind of music
they will never play again.

We played guitar together.
You hated barre chords, loved The Flying Burrito Brothers.
One night we sat on a park bench near the Chicago apartment
and played *Sin City* so slow I thought I'd lose my mind.
We played that song in Miami, Bucharest, Sinaia,
at your office for the Fourth of July and on a train
to Budapest with the Romanians practicing their English.

Some days I listen to that song and feel nothing.
I walk to the grocery store and spend all afternoon
cooking a big dinner for Ed, Beth, and the kids,
taking in the whole Greatest Hits album while chopping onion.
Nothing. That's the thing about grief:
it doesn't hit you until it hits you. It blades the numbness,
quiet, efficient, and sudden as sunlight. The doctor who
calls it *shock* says it might be this way for months,
there are books about it online,
one of her patients—a firefighter—was called out to a house
and didn't think, until months later, the body
he carried out that day could be his daughter.
He fell to pieces. I guess we all do, eventually.

The grief that never entirely wells up or washes away.
It is a kind of sustenance the mind sometimes tries
to digest by consuming all at once,
no matter how shitty the feeling afterward.
Like eating the two-pound burger that gets your photo on the wall
of the local chain restaurant,
it's just not the sort of thing you want to define you.

I keep changing the background picture on my computer,
trying to remember the exact details of whichever day.
Supposedly that's one stage of grief, bartering.
I would exchange any or all of the days ahead
for that afternoon we sat at a bar by your office,
drinking long espressos and waiting for a friend,
when the waiter offered to take the photograph
I've stared at all morning, the old man in a blue suit
and his wife in a red dress passing through,
behind us, shading their faces from the sun.

INDIANAPOLIS

Four Months

In another city the roads face east
beneath trees full of affection for anything
unbound.

Low cloud of mulch, fumes, and sun.
A pasture of stubborn kite-tails.

The dog standing inside the fence
barks sweet loneliness
at a passing mail truck.

ALMANAC

Ten Months

Let's fall in love again. Let's travel again. Let's make ourselves
    uncertain
with the prospects of a new city

again, fly down the freeway to South Florida
or on someone else's dime to South Asia or Eastern Europe again,
make a home for the year somewhere unknown again—

Let's live where the rivers flood the cities every spring again,
or behind the park with the empty lake
boats tied down in the channel for the fall again—

Let's eat too much and walk the whole way home again,
past the Bolivian delis and Ecuadorean patisseries
with glazed sugar chips and candied berries
again, currants in molasses again, espressos light as cream
at the Orthodox-run vegetarian-everything cafe again,
the beer gardens with pizza or the Lebanese joint's
zacusca, lapte, and *mamaliga cu smantana* again—

Let's name everyone but know only each other again,
forget the guidebooks and find the buildings again—

Let's eat Moldovan apples and Turkish baklava
as we walk through Herastrau again,
hike into Busteni and up the mountain again
and let's stop for pictures by the trail marker again—

Let's head over to Jeff and Sheila's and play spades again,
wait outside the apartment for Sarah and Jason again,
take the cable car to get drunk at high altitudes
in Colorado again, or Wallachia again, or Budapest
as the moon rises behind a palace lit up for tourists again,
the seven bridges we cross until we're sure it's Buda again—

Let's leave the market in Istanbul without the plate again,
find the mosque where we watch prayer call again,
on the Friday of my twenty-ninth birthday again—

Let's take all of the years and make them one year again—

Let's live eleven months, six days, and twenty-two hours again
in the city in which I love you again,
in a room that is our home again,
as you walk the steep stairwell and out to the curb again,
and let's not say too much about this or each other again,
for each other because we are each other's again,
this one day that is only one day again.

Tuck Pointing

Three Months

I dig out the black sweater I brought from the home
that is no longer our home the way
you are no longer my wife
and withdraw again into your brother's city
that resembles no place we ever lived together:
blank trees overhanging immaculate lawns,
strip malls with burrito shops and tanning salons,
children who make games with their boredom.
He offers me work as we walk between houses.
He points out the chimneys that need replacing,
how the neighborhood practices neglect.
No piece of this landscape resists our expectations.
Some nights I sit up chewing antacids or cough drops,
thinking how you and I walked across Bucharest
catching up on the smallest details of our time apart.
It was the last time I saw you alive:
yesterday, last night, a few minutes ago.
We spent six years trying to decide what we'd do next.

STORAGE LOCKER

Five Months

Some nights the color is so clean you have to drive it down,
steadying your claim on the potential significance.

Hold the old linen up to the face, a little self-conscious:
one last hit burns like fiberglass in the lungs.

In the hallways of the storage locker there is no uncertainty
about indiscriminate clinging and letting go,
continuing to live as if to make sense of the living.

Hold the oxygen inside until it turns to smoke.
The walls are black. Even the padlock falls away from the key.

Sandwich Notch Road, Two Days Before Christmas

Six Months

On dirt roads
with good friends
the names come back all at once.

No one I know
who lives without deep sorrow.
No one ever
really finished with desire.

The soft animal of my body
does not love
what it has learned.

How could it?

I wind constantly
the fragile timepiece of another life.

No set hour. No luck. No path
that doesn't eventually
double back.

Wanting to live
after your death
is like waking
in an empty room:
too much space.

All day I sleep off
the crude hangover.

THE GATES

Thirty-Nine Months

Every year on the day of your death
I am terrified of light.
A shadow covers your body.
I am tired of trying to say nothing well
to no one in particular,
carefully taking both sides.
The first marriage with the second.
The sky that afternoon, and rain.
The skyline and scaffold of bright fabric
laid over the gate.
We came out the other side
like a magic trick, missing the trick,
one year now six seasons,
a second winter in two cities,
the latter warmer and beginning again
its fog and rain.
I come here in the dark.
I shall leave here in the dark,
you said.
Each step forward
we named something new
that had not changed on either side.

Sleep

Forty Months

Terrific silences organized the room
where I slept after your death.
I was terrified to leave it.
I imagined clearly the hallway
on the other side of the door,
narrow, well-lit, and neatly tiled.
I took a pill, arranged the sheets,
and pulled the room up over my shoulders.
Out of breath I woke between doses
to write down those dreams I remembered.
For quite a while, I talked to someone.
One hour passed, then another
therapist, a different city, sometimes
I tried not to repeat myself
or insist that my grief was ending.

WHEN THE DETECTIVES ARRIVED SUNDAY MORNING

Two Months

I stopped worrying a stranger
would steal your bag from the ridge.

Dispatched to search the sight,
ATVs returned with your blue trail pack,
blue bandanna.

One doctor, then another doctor
with a machine
restated the obvious

while journalists waited
in the hallway to confirm rumors.

I held your arm where it crooked to the body
almost naturally.
Like everyone else I looked at your face.

On the road to the hospital,
pot-holed, slicked, crossed with herds,
the crisp mountain air filled with mosquitoes.

A patrol of state hunters set out to kill a brown bear
with white fur on its paws and chest,
or any bear that night
that happened upon the trail.

LEPIDOPTERA

Eight months

No constellations making shadows on the frozen ground.
No snow raising a monument in the first light.
At the city dump near Kildare and Roosevelt,
last week's recycling wears down its cheap glue
ellipses of green, blue, and yellow ink,
rocket fuel sealing the sky's long envelope.
On television what explodes is the center of anything
finding in the translucence some lifting of the body.
No wings. No one destruction almost balancing the scales.
Transformations fold like fortunes into the ends of the day.
I am waiting out the last hour before you closed the office,
heating water for tea. What will I ever know
of this moment except its place in the sequence?
To set branches beside a fireplace and insist there is no light.
The moon withdraws so the stars make bigger fires.

Rehearsals For Departure

Seven Months

That Easter you flew home to your mother's.
I went with our friends to the basilica
and stood with a candle poked through a Nescafé cup
until the priest announced the Resurrection.
The sun on my neck made an outline along the collar.
I was bored. I was happy
to romanticize your absence.
I kept our routines and resented them,
doing our laundry because it was a Sunday night.
Was it how you wanted to live your last year?
I think you'd resent how the question turns back to me:
It is how we lived our last year, but yes, John,
I wanted to be with you. I obsess your departure
and arrival that spring for some preview of your death.
I log into your email every couple of days
because I can, I guess, but also because I worry
there's someone yet I haven't told,
who will write you to say she misses you.
You kept so few emails.
I've called all of your friends.
The last time I washed your shirts
I folded them like flags and hid them in my closet.

ZUGZWANG

Eighteen Months

(n.) Compulsion to move. *A chess term referring
to a situation in which a player would like to do
nothing (pass), since any move will damage his position.*

Not that it mattered in the beginning
but there were patterns. I saw three moves
to your bishop, six to your rook, nine to your queen
and then a slow game of pawns. Almost at mate,
I forgot the axes running to the corners,
failed to anticipate your casual sweep of the lanes,
one side of my board plucked clean like a branch of wild
anything. You opened a window to let out the heat.
We started again. It felt good to keep playing,
to do one thing well over and over.
Maybe that's why I liked
the pizza place around the block that burnt our crusts,
why you could not wait to move uptown,
away from the martinis, mochas, and Marc Jacobs.
Our new home was several blocks from anywhere.
Half a mile out: a rosary of buoy lights.
If we were quiet and mindful the trees around the lake
shook when we walked beneath them.

THE NEW BEAUTIFUL

Nine Months

When I held your shoulders the city caught fire.
Everything leaned into everything like timber.
I haven't loved you like this for years.

Tell me, again, what we loved about the city
that summer afternoon the balconies went silent,

as you held a camera over the rail and took pictures
of the unfamiliar faces
passing one building, then the next,

like the sound of birds. This wanting the old construction,
the new beautiful
blueprints. Show me what stands in my place.

KATIE GHAZALS

One Year

The magician seemed to promise that something torn to bits might be mended without a seam, that what had vanished might reappear, that a scattered handful of doves or dust might be reunited by a word, that a paper rose consumed by fire could be made to bloom from a pile of ash. But everyone knew that it was only an illusion. The true magic of this broken world lay in the ability of things it contained to vanish, to become so thoroughly lost, that they might never have existed in the first place.

—Michael Chabon,
The Amazing Adventures of Kavalier and Clay

i. Busteni (1)

The corners of the room lampshade every shadow.
Full of answers, they resemble everything.

When the police found your pack I was afraid to open it.
You'd filled it that morning with clothes and books for the week.

I untied from the handle a bandana we'd bought in town that
    morning.
At night it reaches down from the closet shelf like spring growth.

A vine reaching in every direction.
In photos the knapsack is as long as your torso.

Outside the Orthodox chapel: colleagues, friends, priests, a diplomat.
Wreaths of fresh flowers, candle wicks sunk in wax.

The mortician dresses your body in khakis and a silk blouse.
Nothing that we transform becomes you.

I wash your bandana and wear it as I walk without you.
A city that could be any city: unexceptional except for the arriving.

We do it alone, Katie; we mark among the living ghosts of
    those we love.
We never quite make our peace.

ii. Indianapolis (1)

The first time we visited you said your niece drew remarkable horses.
Her sister bit strangers. A nephew would soon turn one.

The biter loved to be thrown in the deep end.
The budding hippologist watched carefully that whole first visit.

Improvising riddles, we entertained the neighbors' kids.
What is the difference between a female wizard and a male witch?

Your brother kept whiskey in the basement with his amps.
Trying the steel, then the Spanish classical; clumsily
    strumming one chord.

Your sister-in-law mixed her signature cocktail, The LaPlantini.
Outsiders to the clan, she and I bonded over movies, books,
    music, *brantówka*.

The biter woke you one afternoon, when Ed and I went to a movie.
So, Katie, is John your boyfriend?

Making good time back to Chicago I always hoped we'd hit traffic.
Car Wheels on a Gravel Road re-starting outside Lafayette.

Tonight, Chase shreds Pat Benatar on *Guitar Hero*.
Beth opens boxes and separates your clothes by size.

We make bundles to take to your sister, her kids, your mother.
Chloe, the biter, and Emma, the hippologist, claim
    sweatshirts; Chase sleeps in your ringer tees.

Later, when the house is quiet, I steal lines from other elegies:
In another room, Kiri Te Kanawa is singing the Laudate
    Dominum of Mozart, very faintly.

iii. Bucharest (1)

An avenue barely wide enough to walk is the shortest route
    through the park.
Three paths round the empty fountain.

The gilt dome of the boathouse shades poplars and pear blossoms.
A basket of warm pretzels wilts yesterday's newspaper.

At the city mausoleum, pigeons spiral the cornices.
Pushed through Nescafé cups, candle wax marks the path of
    mourners.

The cooks at beer gardens pickle their winter salads.
Ceapa, ciuperci, usturoi, soté de morcovi.

Paddleboats in the moonlight shiver and tap like magnets.
The place in you in which the whole universe dwells.

Oolong with jasmine or syrupy dark lager?
Overnight train through the mountains or the morning plain?

Mid-day, Cismigiu Lake is antiseptic green; at sunset, the
    warm tincture of iodine.
Between red and blue tulips, white waxflower.

Tonight, Katie, Cismigiu Lake is black.

iv. Miami

All night, the moon bowls sea-glass under its clockwork tide.
Royal palms swipe their tops at the sea's gummy words.

Water in Miami reaches everywhere; plastic kayaks stocked
    on shelves.
On break, grocery clerks trace cigarettes across the damp
    night's words.

Vinegar and spices soften chicken on the bone.
Wearing down this wood, a cell phone or the ragged click of words?

Downing dollar drafts and nickel wings at the only bar in Kankakee.
C stitched on a wool cap, long in the tooth, wordless.

In 1908 electric coasters looped the provisional city.
A century later a woman collects insurance and cleaves her
    family word by word.

The one Springsteen song Katie liked to sing while driving:
    One Step Up.
A country cover, she taught herself all of the words.

After an ugly fight we sat quietly in the apartment.
You said, *Now, here is the problem with being good at words.*

v. Bucharest (2)

The city is my ancestor.
Perpetual, rebuilt, it discards itself like last year's fashions.

A fire tower shines its irregular beacon across the train yards.
It plays havoc on passing Mercedes and Peugeots.

Near the metro, at night, Soviet-era pensioners beg for spare change.
The accordion players wait outside Pizza Hut.

Teenagers stub cigarettes with silent, careless hands.
Siblings confide in each other and make excuses.

Parents divorce, remarry, make dinner.
Romania joins the EU, so the mayor spends forty million euros.

The prices of beef double in three months.
The British and French buy mountain villas; Germans crowd
   the Black Sea.

Heineken wins the city beer contract.
Through spring, a last impossible keg pours round after round
   of Leffe.

Students practice irony, citing the failures of all revolutions.
The President is impeached and retains his post, a hero to the
   working class.

Beer gardens fill with World Cup enthusiasts.
My first night in the city, you cheer the Italians, boo the Americans.

vi. Busteni (2)

What tends a flame or the space around a flower?
What lifts blossoms from reeds without perpetuating grief?

What attenuates the soul so that it lifts like a prayer?
Who withstands this world not thinking first of grief?

In the clearing, deer measure the distance of passing cars.
Isn't the winter ground, too, only a gesture of grief?

The names of saints linger like these seasons bearing witness.
In any season, they distinguish resurrection and grief.

Among these beatitudes, let there be grace.
Let me sit where we spread your ashes, Katie.

vii. Chicago

Uptown, late autumn, three blocks from our first apartment.
In a side room, the tattoo artist shrugs, *We get a lot of widowers.*

Ink in the skin, rounding the shoulder in slender branches.
A tree with no leaves shades a green apple.

Cut back where an elm over-hangs the path, short grass
    crowds the lake.
Missing one friend's wedding to miss another.

Ivy fills in the outfield walls. The Cubs win six in a row.
All September: hysterical to sing the seventh-inning stretch.

The Kopi Café stocks its signature carrot cake.
This year, on your birthday, it comes topped with a whipped-
    cream carrot.

Anonymous: *Sorrow for a husband is like a pain in the elbow,*
    sharp and short.
Plath: *Widow. The word consumes itself.*

All spring, I wake half a dozen times in the night.
I wait for dreams; in them, I never know what to say.

viii. Fundata

Snow lifted from the ridge all morning and afternoon.
We withstood the cold to take photos.

Home from school, the owner's daughter walked us to the lake.
Near the fence, you lost your shoe in spring mud.

Cheese curds swung from branches; in season, plum brandy.
We spread cured pig fat like butter on fresh bread.

The man who rented cabins kept dogs in a basement pen.
He isolated them from human contact to teach them loyalty.

Through steel fencing: the low howl of indiscriminate need.
Drunk, the owner let us stroke their soft bellies.

At night I hear the ceiling fan whir.
To whom will I testify? Who bears witness to the listening?

ix. Indianapolis (2)

The scent of rain fills this small room beside the garage.
Why sleep all afternoon? Why sleep at all if I return to my body?

Indiana floods. Pumpkin vines poke through the soil.
Chloe weeds her garden and plants our wedding flower by the door.

The old dog: how its diminished hip fills with fluid.
Listing so badly the body can make no accommodation.

Searching the grocery aisles for a box of your favorite crackers.
Panis angelicus fit panis hominum.

Chasing solemn libations with cheap beer.
What could we pour into the soil that will not soak through?

On the wall near my desk we tape ten photographs.
Thunderstorms streak the windows; your brother's house shakes.

The night you died, I held your body, terrified and numb.
There is no arrival or departure; I grieve for everything, Katie.

x. One Year

A climber makes a ridge sacred with her death.
She locates a point of reverence for other journeys.

Where the path curves away from train tracks: your meadow.
We stake a handmade sign that names the place.

Arête: a sharp ridge.
From the Latin *arista:* ear of wheat, fish bone, spine.

A mountain rises noticeably above the surrounding landscape.
The term has no standardized geological meaning; it is generally
    larger than a hill.

Grief: a cycle that seeks no clear resolution.
Your nieces turn handstands on the gravel path and watch for
    snails.

xi. San Francisco

Divinity holds the soul like an ice sculpture; all shape falls away.
One by one, the neighbors return home and curtain their windows.

At the pool, a friend of Ed and Beth's says now is the time to
buy land in the Bay Area.
On a map of the city, I circle neighborhoods near the homes
of friends.

Artillery leveled city blocks to firebreak the 1906 Earthquake.
Unable to channel the sea, they built fire upon fire until it
consumed itself.

There are many names for the logic and power of symbols.
We return to storage your most cherished possessions.

Hidden in the Tea Garden: sculptures and bridges.
I sip oolong with a friend where two paths converge across
the water.

Reading Thich Nhat Hanh, I understand there is no absolute truth.
I accept that sorrow is only one manifestation of love.

In Bangladesh, all summer, we rode night buses through silent
villages.
In monsoon season, on a single-lane highway, the drivers
always made good time.

Driving west, I will cross plains, badlands, hills, mountains, beach.
I will stay with friends in cities we never visited together.

There is no season for grief, no year, no beginning or end to sorrow.
Reverent, when we say your name, love holds the rift a while.

THE
CONSOLATIONS

The Consolations

What Paul wrote about the end,
The day of the Lord will come like a thief in the night
continues *as labor pains on a woman*
meaning, I think, a labor ends.
A woman and a baby return from the hospital,
or the baby dies and the mother lives,
or the mother dies and the baby lives in the arms of a stranger
whose strangeness ends in compassion and habit.
In this way a birth becomes a theft.
A thief becomes sympathetic.
A talented thief who takes something of value
replaces it with a skilled facsimile.
The fact of the thief is the certainty of his absence.
So, perhaps, the day of the Lord is the thief sprung from prison
who cannot decide whether to take or leave the world.
Instead, he returns to his end. When I was a child every spring
a man with a skilled lawyer spoke
at assembly about the burden of an addiction
he carried in the world, the memory of a stranger's headlights
at night's end, the ugly drive all night across a city from one end
of the lane to the other. I thought,
This is the fame of an exception. In the end,
he drives from school to school nursing his pathetic celebrity
so it will not end. Later, a friend skipping classes said
the speaker stopped each time to drink from his water glass
and weep near the end of the speech,
naming his daughter, then the girl's mother,
as though his story could end only with the sober morning,
the jail cell, his crime against the fact of his judgment.
I know that a rite begins with the desire for an end,
as the ritual compels the end,
as the performance of any grief must end

with the continuing life at the memory's end.
Deciding whether or not to live I lived a year in Indiana.
The year came to an end.
I moved to a city in California
the planet has not stopped reshaping into a continent's end.
What I loved about Indiana was how my marriage did not end
so long as I loved my wife's family.
For a while, I wanted nothing to continue after it.
That ended. I was too young for my life to end,
someone said, and someone else said
I was too eager, in the end, to leave Indiana.
Now, the story of a marriage ends only with my wife's death,
then reverence. *Grief does not end*
says the well-meaning stranger at a party
who has nothing
else to say about grief's end.
Perhaps he misses the clarifying intensity of the feeling.
I married again. It felt like committing the very end
of a crime everyone was watching. When my son was born I thought,
The beginning of a family exceeds a marriage's end.
I was lying to myself.
I did not fear for his mother's life.
The tragedy of any death is neither beginning nor end.
The consolation of Paul's epiphany is that his soldier's life
    came to an end.
Grace-struck, he left one town to journey to the next.
Where two mountains ascend in opposite directions from the earth
a valley is named *Consolation*.
Every spring, between rainfalls, bears
lumber from hibernation through the desolate wilderness
and toward a valley. From one side of the river
I imagine calling out at the night's end.
Do I mean still to warn myself?

This is the story I cannot end:
what more than wind and high water diminishes my voice
as I write again and again toward the end of a life
and find no voice to cross it?

YEARS

BEWARE OF ELK

I was happy. I didn't keep a journal.
I rested my head on your shoulder and you kept driving west.
How far since Bozeman? How much further to Utah?
We passed mountains, canyons, and sulfur pools.
We passed buffalo, mountain goats, and squirrels.
In the Gardner River swimming hole
a Korean couple happily scalded their white skin.
Clouds clung like milkweed on the outcrops.
You named widgeons, stills, and rails.
You named sisters, cousins, and aunts.
I said that when your boyfriend left the city that winter
to attend a *Rambo* premiere in Las Vegas,
it gave me hope. How from Dolores Park
a few months later this generous city lit everything:
street cars and pylons, porch-lamps and ships,
the Bay Bridge but not the Golden Gate.
We ate ribs, chicken and brisket.
We drove US-212, State Road 3, I-90.
Crossing the Beartooth Pass the glacial air
was thin and cold and mist rose on the water.
A petrified spruce felled by lightning
peaked the tree line at dusk.
We left Wyoming to enter Yellowstone.
We left the lodge to walk to our cabin.
I don't know how the heart makes decisions.
Maybe love is something born again
in different bodies so it can keep moving forward.
On the wall of a diner just past Heart Lake
rangers nailed simple, hand-painted warnings.
We saw nothing until suddenly, everywhere,
the sound of antlers, like ice chipped from a roof.
It made no sense to count them.

BADLANDS

Theodore Roosevelt came here to die again.
Evenings, rain started from one
side of the sky and crossed overhead.
He named his wife in every miniature valley
peaked with miniature stones.
He slept on floors and under bunks,
democratic, hanging back
when the workmen rushed to work.
Six or seven months he stayed ahead of it,
his fingertips hardening into glass,
the silver on his jacket
translucent from a distance.
He weighted down one name,
then another until they disappeared
from letters: excised, a tax on the work.
He took to trading skins for furs,
rattlesnakes for pop-guns, meat for rope.
Whole afternoons of buffalo
shook the empty ground he crossed.

INCENDIARIES

Only a handful made it to the United States,
some as far as Detroit.
One killed a Sunday school teacher
walking students through the Oregon woods.
However many became rumor,
stuck on power lines near missile silos,
cut into tarps by farmers or chased across the desert
with rifles and pickups,
only seen or heard after the fact
of arrival turned cloud to bulb and flame,
morning and empty field,
it seemed unjust they might keep
the silence of clear skies in their ballast,
burning primitive three-day fuses
sparked by altimeters
if the fuses lit. One capped the snow
while the grass surrounding it grew high stalks.
From the lot where he packed lunches and a tackle box
Pastor Mitchell heard a student yell to his wife,
Look what I found,
the newspapers reported.
He tried to smother the fire on her body.
He followed, fifteen years, the vanishing canopy
and died in a jungle carrying medicine to enemy soldiers.
At the end of the war kamikaze pilots
painted cherry blossoms on their payload.
They took branches from the trees into their cockpits
to deliver the reincarnated souls
of friends and strangers.
Thousands of men *bloomed as flowers of death,*
as high clouds shading the rocky ground
break into pieces and vanish.

ENKIDU: THREE RONDEAU

Shamhat

Old Spice smells like cedar and wild bees.
Old wood never smells like trees.
Old men romp the shape
to hard sugar, score the nape,
then scour their palms in the cold seas.

Whatever you take, please
him. He serves my heart. You frieze
first man in crepe de Chine
of cedar, spice, and wild bees.

No ape would praise creation on clean knees,
though your prayer might ease
such incidental stings and near-escapes.
Roll back the ticker. Seal the tape.
I was man before I learned to name these
cedars, spices and wild bees.

Gilgamesh

I snap trunks, scrap cities, pound beers.
I best men half my years
and twice as big. What virtue astounds
my big heart? I bound
my gypsies in wolf and camel hairs.

I lament my dead with real man-tears.
My sorrow settles all fears.
The gods make light this head they've crowned.
I snap trunks, scrap cities, pound beers.

I am unchanged, year to year.
The woods sway. The earth appears
where sea and sky cannot round
the heavens. We best again the immortal hound.
My best friend disappears.
I snap trunks, scrap cities, pound beers.

Utnapishtim

My grocery cactus leans against the glass,
eager for morning, green as old brass,
certain of the coming light.
Impatient with the slow night,
dim bulbs, and Robert Hass,

the floorboards whine, soft as grass.
All the new thinking is about loss.
My neighbor pulls his shade low and tight.
My grocery cactus leans against the glass.

On 18th Street, night joggers pass and pass,
pious as the Easter Vigil Mass.
Hearty and bright
revelers wobble their top-heavy delight.
The urban air sweetens like cut grass.
My grocery cactus leans against the glass.

BRANCHES

As our plane noses into the clouds over Seoul,
I imagine a boy looking up from a book.
A grackle wings from branch to still branch,
oblivious to the trajectory of my soul miles above,
that is slightly reset by the give of rivets and steel.
He is reading about the history of the universe.
He has stopped to wing pebbles
out across a lake that in the evening light
is the same color as my plane against the sky.
There is no one on the planet but him.
The sound of the ice rejecting each stone
is the sound of his boot soles testing the rim,
is the same creak of turbulence bending the wing
before my body dissolves into a handful of ash
just thick enough to transform the molecules
assembling now as pine and moss and spring
into smoke and something unfamiliar to the boy
who has forgotten the improbability of his solitude
and the origin of numbers he works out exponentially.

BOARDWALK

A man picks up his bicycle from the shop and decides to leave town.
Eight new teeth grip three gears on the back wheel.
The handlebars are yellow, wrapped in blue and orange tassels.
He steers with one hand, admires peaches with the other.
Yellow, under-ripe. Woodblocks balance the crate on both sides.
The city rises in proportion to the lakefront:
low water this time of year, a drought maybe, or just the
    summer heat.
Grass crops the birdbath, the birds muck their feathers,
a crane past the edge leans its boom tip into focus.
Beyond the city, slaughterhouses. Beyond the pig farms,
black soil, a river, two cities, and then another city.
The coast this time of year is warm and dry.
There is a boardwalk three miles from his cousin's home
where a woman he knows sells stereoscopes
of faraway places, old friends, and famous works of art.
Dogs and cats wandering the alley poke their snouts
in the stale compost bins. They sleep all afternoon
beneath concrete props that hold the wood out over the ocean.

You Don't Know What Love Is

All day couples press their bodies against each other
on thin park benches around the lake,
often just young girls straddling their boyfriends,
three or four crowded together beneath the trees,
gossiping while the boys look straight ahead.
How they must concentrate to seem so disinterested!
Or maybe I am too naive to understand the politics
of careful exhibitionism. Or maybe it isn't love at all,
just a kind of rehearsed platonic indifference,
the couples a little further down the path pushing strollers,
stopping at the beer gardens for Cokes and cigarettes.
Their children are young enough to think everyone looks old,
that it's not so bad to grow up to be a fire truck.
They will know, in a few years, the deepest parts of the lake.
Today, love is Sonny Rollins on the headphones
as I pass the sun-bleached pier where the old women
sit watching young boys jump from the bridge.

LEGEND

Filled with carcasses the boat
slips out to sea under its own weight.
A boy is dead. His coat

is blue. His hair is red. His throat,
sharp as a racing skate,
covered in kisses. The boat

should turn quick and straight
into the wind. It doesn't. The boy is eight.
Though dead, his coat

floats three buttons as bait,
one for each day he will wait
to be found. Now, a carcass. Now, the boat

bobs its keel sloppy and low as a waistcoat
drags cumbersome freight
toward a simple end. The footnote

is some moral. Know what you love. Write
with care the suffering child in the bloody crate.
Load carcasses into the boat.
Kill the boy in his summer coat.

AUBADE

I watch you out of habit,
which is to say, without purpose

at this hour, when everything is useless,
even socket plugs, gates, and cabinet locks.

They shine their neon logic to caution
the dark room. In a few hours,

we'll bring the bottle, open curtains,
look at books, dress for the day.

You'll wear shorts and a hoodie
with a dinosaur on the back

to make you strong.
I'll say you are my boy and mean it

is impossible to deny all of you,
hair-shocked, semi-coherent, somewhat eager

to find and test the world
again, to survive need and want.

Around your eyes, you are your mother.
You have my high forehead and stubborn streak.

It's warm tonight, a little humid.
I should get back to bed

before you wake and see me.
Roll toward the middle,

away from the sharp slats,
if you can. Sleep until morning.

ORCHARD

We might learn to expect it to bear fruit
again each summer if only
that so many pies, crisps, and cakes, chutneys and butters
extend one season past the next.
And when you reach from the porch with a picker
I stand in the driveway with the basket doing my best
to will a trajectory. Let me finish what you start.
Please trust me to do it well.
There is a five-second rule for any fruit, however bruised.
We peel it almost to the core to salvage it.
We clamp the corer to the table and turn hundreds
of sour ribbons, sweetening
the compost pile next to the laundry line.
In Indiana a niece prepares her spring garden.
She turns the hard dirt under the dryer's exhaust
and tacks to the wall a six-week schedule:
squash and beefsteak tomatoes,
then corn, beets, and sweet potatoes.
Land is the occasion to work, lament
the seasons, and pray for rain
is the mindset I tried and failed to bring West.
Here, everything grows until it becomes something else
again. My niece harvests three small banana peppers
her mother eats with oil and fresh bread,
singing her praises. All summer, her garden does not grow
while our yield diminishes in milk crates and baskets.
At night, coyotes and the snap
of branches, bobbing their lost weight,
pitch songs of relief past our incomprehension.
The moon rises past the coastal hills, toward Indiana.

In the cool kitchen you press your thumb
under and across a paring knife,
piling slices, harvesting fire
where lines of alternating light and dark
pull the world into and through our temporary home.

DIRT

Forget the bent whistle rattling its pebble
well past the shape of its tone,

the metal detector and the confederate bullet,
the ivy, gunmetal, brick.

It is winter. The evening light diminishes,
littered with false starts.

Black-shouldered kites wing redwoods,
quartering grasslands for rabbits and mice.

The Japanese maple bares thick branches.
Who doesn't wait for the ground to surrender

some aspect of what was set beneath it
waits for spring. Fermented holly berries

thrill the blackbirds. The reservoir is low.
On the hill, beneath a satellite dish

too old to hear much among the constellations,
joggers crowd the familiar route.

YOUNG WIDOWER

There is a moment at the beginning of your new marriage
when it bugs you that your new wife
still uses the email address with her maiden name.
Didn't you get married again to clear up such confusions?
You can try this at home. Drive into the middle of a park.
Drive a spade into the soil around the largest tree
until the tip comes up covered in blood.
You have to drive the tool right through the thick
fur of ground rodents to leave a mark.
Out on a bike ride, some chipmunk or squirrel
shakes the entire hedge trying to scurry away
from your fat tire. It makes sense to live in fear of pain
about as much as your dead wife's brother suddenly
loves rock-climbing. What were you thinking,
running down some helpless creature
minding her own business, indifferent to you?
Your first wife, she wanted nothing more than to shed
the dead weight of your name that clicked,
like a busted shoulder, every time she tried to use it.

TRAVEL

I can see flaws where the photo is worn,

the lush trees dulled with autumn
robbed of their chlorophyll.

My white arm on your shoulder
is no darker than the temple behind us,
which we never entered.

Your hair matches the roof.

Ten years, I waited to know this moment
intimately. It wasn't waiting

but wanting that kept
whole cities between us.

How I loved so much distance
I can only imagine.

Four Romanian Proverbs

Cine Te Vede Intrând în cârciumă Nu Zice Că Ai Intrat Să Te închini.
Anyone who sees you walking in the pub won't think that you're there to pray.

In the early 1950s,
to honor renaming the city Oraşul Stalin,

forestry officials in Brasov set controlled burns,
then planted a crop of fir trees
so that the shape of *STALIN*
was clearly visible from the city center.

The night of his death
a mob of citizens worked dusk-til-dawn secretly
chipping away at the green wood.

Now, in winter, only the last four letters are visible.

Not that Stalin would care. He visited so few
of the places named for him.

Among all of the titles he accumulated around the world—
Coryphaeus of Science, Father of Nations,
Brilliant Genius of Humanity,
Gardener of Human Happiness—
the imprint lingers locally like a cipher,
far more dangerous and subtle than the message it contains.

It took him four days to die. His daughter said
his left hand lifting suddenly brought down a final curse.

The body's last reaction to rat poison?
Bad ham? Too much vodka, stress, and old age?

Who knows. The politburo ordered an autopsy
but no doctor in his right mind would cut on Uncle Joe.

Cine S-a Fript Cu Ciorba, Suflă şi-n Iaurt
He who burns his tongue in soup will blow in yogurt too.

We reverse the spell in inches,
line by line,
until the code itself is indecipherable:

charcoal sparks on the pavement,
tarnish greening the church spires,
the river low at evening tide.

The old woman selling tin half-dollars
imports jasmine and sandalwood incense,
healing stones, swords, chestnut beer.

She points to the exact bills you should hand her.
Her prices are not inflated.
No one barters. No one even talks.

Her system is closed for foreigners
who do not want to be foreigners.
The dollar loses a third of its value in four months.

One year later you never speak the language.
Your lack of fluency amuses but does not surprise
colleagues. They speak English to you,

Romanian to each other,
French to their students,
German at the British night school.

The slow acid of conversion wears down,
even as the intention is clear and unremarkable,
portable, navigated, stilled.

We are Byron without the fever.
Our climax is just another cliffhanger chapter,
Missolonghi, or How I Escaped Intact!

Buturuga Mică Răstoarnă Carul Mare.
The small log can overthrow the big cart.

Spring comes to Bucharest through open windows,
without air-conditioning, as I sit for hours watching men
play backgammon in the storefront shade.

In a hot room cold beer is magnificent.
It is every last quarter counted out from a tin can.
It is an abundance of hot water now that everyone showers cold.

At night mosquitoes, flies, and moths seek out lamps
and the radiance of warm bodies in these rooms.
I ramp up the internal thermostat and sweat sweet Leffe,

waking up in the morning with nary a bite.
My American colleague explains that Romanians suffer
less from infestation because they still spray DDT.

I've started checking his sources.
He lies a lot. Or, if he doesn't lie, he stretches
each fact until it resembles its opposite.

He is a walking mirror, the sort of guy
you see too much of yourself in if you get too close.
But he's right about the DDT, the lead in the water pipes,

the carcinogenic potential of sugar-free Coca-Cola.
He tells his fifth graders they can stop taking multivitamins
if they just switch to beer. Drink for drink. Better carbs, too.

Cine Sapă Groapa Altuia Cade Singur In Ea.
He who digs another man's grave ends up falling in it.

Lake-effect snow swirls; the real stuff sticks.
Wind off Lake Michigan spirals through the skyline,
finds a place to enter and leave and enter again,

bowing stop signs, glazing the corner slush,
snapping pellets against industrial windowpanes
with all the permanence of keys clacking out

notices past due. Ours is a perpetual debt
of languages, characters, gestures, implications.
The profit is collective and distributed top-down.

Buildings aspire to height rather than volume,
as though the sun at any moment might stop shining
all the way down to commuters in heavy coats.

BABY DUCKS

Fragile as epiphytes,
tight as silk saris or orange peels:
the truth always gives way.

The day we met
I convinced you I overcame
childhood rickets. Later:
that I flew with John Denver
the night before he died.

Here's a fact:
95% of baby fowl
purchased each Easter
never make it to their first birthday.

Forgive all of this
confessing—

but when I told you
if it gets bad
to think of baby ducks
I didn't love you. Not like this.

Round And Round

I'll tell you something—I fucking hate the 90's.
—Mickey Rourke, *The Wrestler*

Even the beautiful are mismatched improbably on the big screen.
No one finds love. Everyone accepts as dogma the unitary potential
of music from the decade after their birth. Heartache
rattles the varnish like someone dropping a quarter through it.
There is no bar down the street where Cait and I will shoot pool
after a big fight. There will be no big fight. I want simple,
simple love. When the wrestler leans away from the stripper,
he becomes for an instant Mickey Rourke insisting
It's me, America. I'm all better now.
I won't ever make you sit through Angel Heart again.
The conditional only works if the corollary is plausible.
Walter Mattheau said the difference between
winning an Oscar and not winning an Oscar is that they carve
He Won An Oscar on your gravestone. When I was seven
my dad and I tossed a baseball. Now he won't put down the phone.
I'm terrified of small children eager to throw hard objects.
Use your words. That's what Cait's older sister told her youngest
as he screamed and pointed at the plate of cold spaghetti.
Everyone agrees the movie about the illiterate Nazi masochist
nurse will win this year's Oscar. There's a menace in affection,
a mendacity in the elegant repetition of simple actions,
is what I tell myself I'm thinking as Marisa Tomei
bends low to the ground, backwards, to receive dollar bills.

REMARRIED

It was beautiful those early winters in Miami,
dew on the hoods of cars in the garage,
gasoline glossing mowers.
I cannot tap this part of our life for misery,
I don't think. You would come home
on the late bus or we would meet
halfway and walk together
through the mangrove, down 151st Street.
Your mother keeps a photo of that kitchen
on her mantle and what I say
about marriage hasn't much changed.
If you are well enough alone, I live.
If you were mine to live alone after, I wasted us,
curving time and space toward my center
so I might run you on rails,
the track smooth and curling like paper at the edge
of a fire. I turned us in one direction.
I wanted injury or correction to end that life
that ended instead with your death.
There was a middle point between two marriages
where I could not remain inconsolable.
What was left to resist except *our*
becoming *my,* then *you?*
I layered grief and happiness loose and close to my skin,
grateful for the warmth. Say it was fast. I leaned
into love and held at a distance the shrug of my shadow.

THE LEGEND OF A LIFE

Five Years

> There is a mountain in the distant West
> That, sun-defying, in its deep ravines
> Displays a cross of snow upon its side.
> —Longfellow, *The Cross of Snow*

Your name is written on paper in a folder
in a shoebox in the closet,
on my arm above the shoulder,
next to a tree near an outcrop of rocks
where we carried your body toward the ridge and stopped to rest.
What does it really matter now how well I tell the story
of my own terrible exception to your death?
I don't know that we ever meant to leave you in one place
but I have spent five years trying to do it.
On grassland in Northern Illinois
we spread your ashes. I go there once a year.
Somewhere between Chicago and Antioch I find the preserve,
frontage road and parking lot.
Close to the quarter-mile turn grasses grow in patterns
less distinct each spring. I guess the place.
I have taken my son there twice.
I have walked him to where we cannot find your body
so he will learn reverence for another life
he knows is some part of this one,
built between places where the earth holds in its fire
and the light at the top of each radio tower blinks red to warn
high travellers looking down.
The city windows shine hills back.
My jacket is blue. It makes no reflection.

I keep my vigil though no gentle face watches down
the unfamiliar room. My clean, fat face
young enough still and fairly circumspect,
impresses perhaps some partial and familiar caricature.
We slept in a small apartment facing west toward the river.
That other time so close to our beginning,
now your end. Not this life,
my second marriage. My later life.
The dust ground low the down incline
as though it were noble only to live that other way,
self-impressed in granite: a clean, hard face.
I remember you now as that life, that other place.
When I say *you* I mean the many sad and beautiful things
that persist after your death,
filings following the magnet-fork,
logical and duty bound to drag without intention
the sloppy figure-eight. Round and round,
I scrape some lost charge against the wood to shape my sad story,
my beautiful wife, my legend,
I might still remember and love you
these beautiful spring mornings I wake early with the baby,
when I let my wife, your friend, climb back into bed
to sleep in our city on the peninsula.
I love this life *after you*
like a stranger arriving late to his own surprise party, stubborn
with disbelief, eager to make up lost time,
each year thinking, *love more,*
whatever the deceit, however obvious or cowardly or sad
I claim the affection. This beautiful spring city.
In the park my son scales the yellow-red play structure
in one direction and leans out, ready to jump.
He is named for my great-uncle, his family's profit: all black wool.
He wore a white hat with a flower in its brim
to persuade the skeptics who did not also speak in tongues.
He made his post-war fortune buying surplus cargo trains,

sending home soccer balls and macadamia nuts
as though he'd found the rest of the world
in the feeding troughs and holding pens of the Central Valley.
California: land of milk and honey, sun and pasture
bordered with snow west and north
of the long flat plain, the deep ravine breaking rivers,
the mountain valleys peaked with snow and filled with bears.
I stood beside a glacial lake,
thinking *I'll see it here. I'll die here. They will find me here.* I
    slept under a blanket
in a cabin in the woods. I drove to the city
and woke early each morning,
the waking memories sudden and tedious as waking.
Say it gets better or there is another kind of end to it.
No feral dog-packs range, bear-hungry, to keep me safe,
the way a fever burns to the center
and kills what it crosses.
Made benedight by history and circumstance
the city's stone horsemen gallop toward fire and rapture
and do not cross it
again. They have already crossed it. Their names are written in stone.
I rode gallant out of Damascus and spoke in tongues.
I was struck without sight or speech or hunger
three days times three and six and ten. I did not die.
I was not converted.
My name is not the name of my son.
I drove west across my country, away from you.
Where will I ever look to discover suddenly that cross's shadow,
knowing I want to see it
across the strait: narrow pasture.
Further: white windmills,
the glacial pass closed half the year to traffic.
Rain slightly warmer than the ocean hides the city.
It gathers to high ice in the winter light.
We hiked six hours to that beautiful ridge.

A cross at the trailhead faced southeast from the valley.
There is no reason to tell this story again.
It is no longer my story.
I know better than to look for consolation.
I make my testament in order to leave you
far from anywhere I might go again.
I catch my son and carry him up the steps.
I run the steps, a foolish running man,
an old man who skips steps, eager for the top,
eager to feel atop
whichever part of the continuing life I cannot stop
remaking. Fog clods the sea high overhead.
My wife is waking now. My son
wants to be lifted high and carried across the city.

NOTES

"Eclogue"
> The italicized text is condensed from the end of John Sullivan Dwight's 1855 English choral translation of Placide Cappeau's "Cantique de Noël."

"Almanac"
> In Romanian: *zacusca* (roasted eggplant vegetable spread), *lapte* (milk), and *mamaliga cu smantana* (polenta with sour cream). Herastrau is the name of a lake and park in northern Bucharest. Wallachia is the historical geographic region in which Bucharest is situated. Busteni is the name of the city from which Katie and I hiked, to the mountain on the day she died. The thirty-third line borrows from the title of Li Young-Lee's *The City in Which I Love You*, with reference to the long poem, "The Cleaving."

"Sandwich Notch Road, Two Days Before Christmas"
> The eleventh line is addressed specifically, and the poem generally, to Mary Oliver's poem, "Wild Geese."

"The Gates"
> The seventeenth and eighteenth lines are from Michael Longley's poem, "The Quilt."

"Rehearsals for Departure"
> The title is taken from the 1999 album and song by Damien Jurado.

"The Katie Ghazals"
> The last line of *ii. Indianapolis (1)* is from Donald Hall's elegy for Jane Kenyon, "How Could She Not." In Romanian: *brantówka* (vodka distilled from fermented mash).

The tenth line of *iii. Bucharest (1)* is Ram Dass's explanation of the meaning of the word, "Namaste." In Romanian, *ceapa* (onion), *ciuperci* (mushroom), *usturoi* (garlic), *soté de morcovi* (sautéed carrots).

The eleventh line of *vii. Chicago* is an unattributed English proverb; the twelfth line is the first line of Sylvia Plath's poem, "Widow."

The eighth line of *ix. Indianapolis (2)* is the first line of Thomas Aquinas's hymn, "Sacris Solemniis." It is translated to English as, "The bread of angels becomes the bread of man."

The eighth line of *x. One Year* is the 2011 online Encyclopedia Britannica's definition of "mountain."

"The Consolations"
The opening lines attributed to Paul are from chapter 5 of his first epistle to the Thessalonians in the King James translation of the New Testament.

"Beware of Elk"
The poem makes a rough chronology of my drive west from Indiana to California.

"Badlands"
Theodore Roosevelt refused to publicly (and often, privately) acknowledge his first wife, Alice, after her death, even to his daughter, who was her namesake. Roosevelt also makes no mention of Alice in his *Autobiography* and in his published letters. Alice Roosevelt died shortly after giving birth to their daughter. It is unclear whether her pregnancy masked the symptoms of Bright's disease, or if she died from complications after childbirth. After Alice's death, Roosevelt journeyed west to the Badlands. Two and

a half years later, Roosevelt married Edith Carow,
his teenage sweetheart, with whom he had five more
children.

"Incendiaries"
On May 5, 1945, Reverend Archie Mitchell and his
pregnant wife led a picnic for Sunday school children
near Bly, Oregon. As he gathered groceries in the
parking lot, his wife called out from the woods, *Look
what I found.* She and the children were instantly killed
by an incendiary balloon. It had drifted into the woods,
unexploded, several months earlier, from Japan. Two and
a half years later, Pastor Mitchell and his second wife
sailed to Indo-China to work as medical missionaries.
In 1962, Viet Cong guerillas seized the hospital where
Mitchell and his family lived and worked. Mitchell
traded medical supplies and his own captivity for the
guarantee of his family's safety. He and two colleagues
were taken hostage and never released.

"Enkidu: Three Rondeau"
The seventh line of *Utnapishtim* is the first line of
Robert Hass's poem, "Meditation at Lagunitas."

"Legend"
The poem is addressed, with concern, to Jason Brown's
short story, "Afternoon of the Sassanoa."

"Four Romanian Proverbs"
The proverbs were collected from students at George
Cosbuc National College, an English-language high
school in Bucharest, Romania, between 2006 and
2007. Thanks to those students for their help with the
translations, as well as with understanding some of the
less obvious colloquial meanings.

"Round and Round"

The epigraph is from Darren Aronofsky's film, *The Wrestler* (2008).

ACKNOWLEDGMENTS

Grateful acknowledgment is made to the following publications for poems that originally appeared in them (although, in some cases, in different form):

The Missouri Review: "Eclogue," "Scale" *(Poem of the Week, 10/14/10)*, "When the Detectives Arrived Sunday Morning," "Boardwalk," "Round and Round," "There Are No Words," "The New Beautiful"

ZYZZYVA: "The Consolations," "Legend," "Aubade"

Slate: "Sandwich Notch Road, Two Days Before Christmas"

The Gettysburg Review: "Almanac"

The Southern Review: "Part-Time"

Epoch: "Beware of Elk"

Michigan Quarterly Review: "Tuck Pointing"

Best New Poets 2006: "Zugzwang"

Northwest Review: "Buturuga Mică Răstoarnă Carul Mare," "Cine S-a Fript Cu Ciorba, Suflă şi-n Iaurt," "Cine Te Vede Intrând în cârciumă Nu Zice Că Ai Intrat Să Te închini"

Blackbird: "Young Widower," "Sleep"

Arroyo Literary Review: "Remarried," "The Gates," "Rehearsals for Departure"

Poetry Northwest: "Lepidoptera"

The Cincinnati Review: "Storage Locker," "Branches"

H_NGM_N: "You Don't Know What Love Is"

Poetry Daily: "Eclogue," "Scale"

Hayden's Ferry Review: "i. Busteni (1)," "ii. Indianapolis (1)," "vii. Chicago," "ix. Indianapolis (2)," "xi. San Francisco"

Fogged Clarity: "Incendiaries"

Tigertail: "iv. Miami"

Verse Daily: "Cine S-a Fript Cu Ciorba, Suflă şi-n Iaurt"

Mantis: "Baby Ducks"

B O D Y: "Enkidu: Three Rondeau"

Some of the poems appear in the chapbooks *No Season* (FWQ, 2011) and *Zugzwang* (RockSaw, 2009).

Many thanks to the Creative Writing Program at Stanford University for its generous support, and for the gift of time, during the writing of this book.

Thanks also to Mihaela Moscaliuc and to Trio House Press, especially Dorinda Wegener, for understanding this book, recognizing it, and working with me to make its place in the world.

Special thanks to Eavan Boland, for her continuing encouragement, help, and example, and to Ken Fields, who made a welcome space among strangers for many of these poems when I had very little confidence in them.

My gratitude to those writers who gave such helpful edits,

in particular Ben Hubbard, Stephanie Wooley-Larrea, Joshua Rivkin, James Arthur, L.S. McKee, Joe Clifford, Kelly Luce, Hannah Haas, Maria Hummel, to the Raffel Family Foundation Braintrust, and to my colleagues at Stanford.

Thanks to my parents, my siblings and their families, my friends, Katie's family, and Ed and Beth and Emma and Chloe and Chase, for making the world whole after Katie's death.

In memoriam, Katie Evans (1976-2007).

About the Author

John W. Evans was born in Kansas and grew up in New York and Chicago. His memoir, *Young Widower* (University of Nebraska Press, 2014), won the 2013 River Teeth Book Prize. His poems and essays appear in *Slate, The Missouri Review, Boston Review, ZYZZYVA, The Rumpus,* and *Poetry Daily,* as well as the chapbooks, *No Season* (FWQ, 2011) and *Zugzwang* (RockSaw, 2009). After completing a Wallace Stegner Fellowship in poetry, John was a Jones Lecturer at Stanford University, where he continues to teach creative writing today. He has worked as a Peace Corps volunteer in Bangladesh, a public school teacher in Chicago, and a college teacher in Romania. He lives in Northern California with his wife and two young sons.

About the Artist

Rachel Burgess was born in Boston, MA. She holds a B.A. in Literature from Yale University and an M.F.A. in Illustration from the School of Visual Arts. Her work exhibits nationally and internationally in galleries and museums, and also features in books and magazines. She has been recognized by publications such as *CMYK Magazine, the Society of Illustrators Annual,* and *3x3 Magazine of Contemporary Illustration*; she is also the recipient of several awards.

Artist Statement:
My work explores loss and gain through depictions of my native New England. I am interested in the way in which the ache of nostalgia is balanced by its ability to reveal patterns in our lives, providing a sense of continuity in a world where visual information is so often overwhelming.

I draw inspiration from classical Western illustration and traditional Japanese prints and paintings; I am also influenced by the mutable yet consistent quality of folk narratives and oral tradition. On a formal level, I use monotype because the process mirrors my interest in loss and gain, as the "painting" that I create on a plate is erased and a unique print on paper is created.

Websites:
www.rachel-burgess.com (official site)
www.facebook.com/rachelburgessart (Facebook)
www.twitter.com/RachBurgessArt (Twitter)

About the Book

The Consolations was designed at Trio House Press
through the collaboration of:

Dorinda Wegener, Lead Editor
Rachel Burgess, Cover Art: *After the Rain*
Dorinda Wegener, Cover Design
Matt Mauch, Cover Design Assistant
Lea Deschenes, Interior Design

The text is set in Adobe Caslon Pro.

The publication of this book is made possible, whole or in part,
by the generous support of the following individuals and/or agencies:

Anonymous

About the Press

Trio House Press is a collective press. Individuals within our organization come together and are motivated by the primary shared goal of publishing distinct American voices in poetry. All THP published poets must agree to serve as Collective Members of the Trio House Press for twenty-four months after publication in order to assist with the press and bring more Trio books into print. Award winners and published poets must serve on one of four committees: Production and Design, Distribution and Sales, Educational Development, or Fundraising and Marketing. Our Collective Members reside in cities from New York to San Francisco.

Trio House Press adheres to and supports all ethical standards and guidelines outlined by the CLMP.

The Editors of Trio House Press would like to thank Mihaela Moscaliuc.

Trio House Press, Inc. is dedicated to the promotion of poetry as literary art, which enhances the human experience and its culture. We contribute in an innovative and distinct way to American Poetry by publishing emerging and established poets, providing educational materials, and fostering the artistic process of writing poetry. For further information, or to consider making a donation to Trio House Press, please visit us online at: www.triohousepress.org.

Other Trio House Press Books you might enjoy:

Flight of August by Lawrence Eby
      2013 Louse Bogan Winner selected by Joan Houlihan

The Ghosts of Lost Animals by Michelle Bonczeck Evory, 2013

Fellow Odd Fellow by Steven Riel, 2013

Clay by David Groff
      2012 Louse Bogan Winner selected by Michael Waters

Gold Passage by Iris Jamahl Dunkle
      2012 Trio Award Winner selected by Ross Gay

If You're Lucky Is a Theory of Mine by Matt Mauch, 2012

CPSIA information can be obtained at www.ICGtesting.com
Printed in the USA
LVOW07s0810250215

428295LV00005B/513/P